The Three Wishes

A traditional tale from England retold and dramatised as a scripted play for five readers.

Ellie Hallett

This story works well as simultaneous reading for groups of five as 'out loud' classroom reading.

It is also suitable as a stage performance.

For more information about *The Three Wishes* when performed as a play, please refer to the end of this book.

Have Fun!

S 1	Once upon a time there was a poor Woodcutter and his Wife. They lived in a tumble-down cottage at the edge of a pine forest. While the pile of bills was growing higher day by day, the coins in the money-jar were becoming fewer and fewer. One day the Wife spoke to the Woodcutter in a very cross voice.

Wife	I'm not at all happy, Husband. In fact, I'm very annoyed. We have only enough money for a few more days. Take your axe and chop down a large leafy tree today to sell for timber, unless, of course, you want us both to starve to death.
Wood cutter	Of course not, Wife! Sometimes I think your sharp tongue will get us into all sorts of trouble.
S 2	The woodcutter and his wife were not to know how much trouble was in store because of this sharp tongue.
S 1	Let us see what happens next. This Wife was a grumpy woman 24/7, and today was no exception.

Wife	Here is a sandwich for your lunch, Husband. It's dry bread and mouldy cheese, but I can't make gourmet from last week's leftovers. Make sure you sharpen you axe or you'll take all day. And now, pray tell, what is your tree-chopping plan?
Wood cutter	Well, I noticed a fine oak in amongst the ordinary pinewood trees the other day. I have never seen it before because oak doesn’t usually grow around here.
Wife	An oak? You've always talked about finding a oak. Maybe you'll be able to earn good money at last instead of putting us both in the poor house.

Wood cutter	And, I might add, it was such a fine tree that it would give enough sweet wood to make hundreds of carvings to sell at the market. That money jar of yours will then be filled right to the very top!
S 2	The thought of having a full money jar made the wife's eyes light up just for a second before she started being cross and bossy once again.
Wood cutter	I've already harnessed up Bessie …
Wife	Oh for crying out loud! Yes, yes, you've harnessed old Bessie. So, what are you waiting for, Husband? Get a move on. And don't come back here without your precious oak tree!

S 1	So off went the Woodcutter and Bessie. The Woodcutter's plan was to chop down the oak tree and Bessie would then drag the big log home.
S 2	The Woodcutter was just about to start chopping when a very small man dressed in bright green jumped down from the branches of the oak tree.
Wood cutter	My goodness! You gave me an awful fright, and I almost trod on you! Wait a minute! You are small enough to be an elf, but my wife says there are no such people as elves or goblins or fairies and all that nonsense. Could you please explain to me who you are and what you are doing?

Elf	Certainly. To clarify your confusion, I am indeed an elf. And by the look of that large axe, you are a Woodcutter. I hope you aren't planning to chop my oak down.
Wood cutter	You guessed right. I am a Woodcutter, and I have orders from my wife to find the biggest and best tree in the forest and chop it down. This oak is it!
Elf	Oh please don't cut down this tree! My home is right up there in the uppermost branches. And what do you think will happen to all the birds and animals and insects that also live here if this tree is chopped down?

Wood cutter	Well, Mr Elf – I am poor, and my wife will be even crosser than usual if I don't fill her money jar from the wood carvings I will make and sell. Please try to see my side of the problem.
Elf	*(said enthusiastically)* All right! I can see that we are facing not one but two problems. I have an idea … *(said slowly and importantly)* I will grant you three wishes if you don't chop this oak tree down. Think carefully. You are being given not one, not two, but three wishes! A very generous offer, you must agree.
Wood cutter	Mmmm. Three wishes! You mean I can wish for anything I like?

Elf	Yes. Anything your heart desires! Consider what you and your good lady wife could have with three wishes. Gold, diamonds, a beautiful house or anything you care to name.
Wood cutter	Gold, diamonds, a beautiful house? *(thinks)* Why thank you, Mr Elf. This could be a win-win situation. You stay in your oak tree and I'll have enough money to keep my, *ahem*, good lady wife happy.
S 1	The Elf shook the Woodcutter's hand to seal the deal. Back into the oak tree went the Elf to tell the birds and animals and insects the good news.

S 2	The Woodcutter was very excited about the three wishes and the prospect of being not just rich, but **very** rich. He and Bessie went home with wings on their feet.
Wood cutter	Wife! Wife! You'll never believe what happened today!
Wife	Husband! Whatever is the matter? I haven't seen you this excited since our old cow Hettie had a calf.
Wood cutter	This is *much* better than Hettie having a calf. In fact, it is much better than anything you have ever heard in your whole long life!

Wife	Well, out with it man! Can't you see I am busy trying to mend one of your old shirts. Tell me this so-called good news and then I'll go back to my stitching. And pass me those scissors while you're at it.
Wood cutter	There is no easy way to tell you, dear wife, but an Elf in the forest gave me three wishes to stop me cutting down his oak tree. Just think what we can do with three wishes! Gold, diamonds, a bcautiful house.
Wife	What did you just say? Surely I misheard you. You did **what**?

Wood cutter	It sounds impossible, I know, but you must believe me because ...
Wife	Let me get this straight, Husband. What do you mean, an elf? Don't tell me you have fallen for some fancy story from a stranger. Anyway, as I've said many times before, there's no such thing as an elf! Or, for that matter, a lucky wish.
Wood cutter	It's hard to believe, I know. But at last we have the chance to be rich and happy for a change. No more darning my shirts or looking in the money jar to see if we have enough to buy food. Think how our lives are about to change!

Wife	Huh! I'll believe it when I see it. Wishes that come true indeed. Huh! And talking about food, I am **so** hungry, I wish I could have a big plate of sausages!
S 1 and S 2	**Whoosh!** *(A large plate of sausages appears as the wife pulls away a cloth on the table in front of her.)*
S 1	But this is where the trouble really starts, as you will soon see.
S 2	It is hard to know who received the biggest shock – the woodcutter or his bad-tempered wife.
Wood cutter	Oh my goodness! These wishes are real! You foolish woman. Do you realise what you have just done?

Wife	Stop grumbling! So, ha ha ha, one of your silly wishes has come true.
Wood cutter	You've just used one of our three precious wishes on a plate of silly old sausages, and *(prodding sausages with his fingers)* and, they aren't even cooked!
Wife	*(getting angry)* I don't want sausages. I want a new house and new dresses and diamond rings and lots of expensive things. Oh, I'm so cross, *(stamps foot)* I wish one of those sausages was, was, was stuck to the end of your nose! *(While the wife has been talking, the Woodcutter has turned his back and quickly attached a sausage to the end of his nose.)*
S 1 and S 2	**Whoosh!**

Wood cutter	Oh no! **Now** look what you've done. A raw sausage is stuck to the end of my nose **and**, you've used another wish.
Wife	Don't worry! I'll pull it off and we'll still have one wish left. Come here, you silly husband with a silly sausage on the end of your silly nose! For goodness sake – stand still. *(pulls and grunts with the effort)* I'll have it off in no time at all and then we can make a proper wish! Stand **still**, I said!
S 1	But no matter how hard they both pulled and tugged and tugged and pulled, that sausage would not budge from the end of the Woodcutter's nose.

Wood cutter	**Ouch!** That hurts. Stop pulling. Oh, I can't stand this sausage on the end of my nose. And – it's starting to smell. *(Sniffs and makes a face as if the sausage is starting to smell. Wife also has a sniff up close to the sausage and pulls a face.)*
Wife	You'll just have to put up with it, husband. Stop fussing! I'm now going to wish for a huge three-storey house with six bedrooms, a swimming pool, a hundred new dresses, two hundred shoes and …
Wood cutter	*(urgently)* Wife – stop, stop! How can I live in a big house with a smelly sausage dangling from my nose? Think how many dogs will follow me around all day if I stay like this!

Wife	*(thinks for a moment)* But what about the big house, the swimming pool and my hundred dresses? Oh botheration! I suppose you're right. I certainly don't want a husband with a smelly sausage hanging from his nose. What would the neighbours say! Oh! It's too awful to think about.
Wood cutter	So how do you think I feel? No – I'm afraid that's the end of our beautiful dream to be rich. *(pause)* I wish that this smelly sausage was off the end of my nose! *(Woodcutter spins around, removing the sausage)*
S 1 and S 2	**Whoosh!**

S 2	And with that, the sausage vanished off the end of the Woodcutter's nose.
Wood cutter	*(crying loudly)* What a waste of three beautiful wishes!
Wife	No wishes, no new house, no diamonds, no gold! *(also cries loudly)*
S 1	All the Woodcutter and his Wife had left was a plate of smelly sausages.
S 2	However, this story doesn't end here.
S 1	It certainly doesn't.
S 2	The woodcutter's wife often lost her temper, but not quite as frequently.
S 1	She eventually learnt to bite her tongue before cross words came out.

S 2	The woodcutter was able to make carvings from ordinary pine wood.
S 1	He knew that his carvings would never be as beautiful as ones made with oak, but he made quite a comfortable living.
S 2	The most unusual part of this story is how it ends.
S 1	Although he looked in every part of the forest, the Woodcutter was unable to find that oak tree ever again.
S 2	Nor did he ever see the little elf.
All	And so ends the famous story of The Three Wishes!

Information for *The Three Wishes* when performed as a play.

Cast

Woodcutter	dressed in casual clothes and carrying an axe
Elf	dressed in elfin clothes
Wife	with blackened eyebrows, red cheeks and frown lines
Two Storytellers	each wearing a hat labelled Storyteller 1 Storyteller 2

Props (optional)

Axe	for woodcutter - made from painted card or balsa wood
Sausages	pantyhose tubes filled with cotton wool, newspaper, old rags or similar
Sticky tape	for attaching sausage to nose
Small table and plate	for sausages
Cloth	to cover sausages (tea towel or small tablecloth)

The Readers' Theatre series by Ellie Hallett

These **Readers' Theatre** stories have a major advantage in that everyone has equal reading time. Best of all, they are theatrical, immediately engaging and entertaining. Ellie Hallett's unique play-in-rows format, developed and trialled with great success in her own classrooms, combines expressive oral reading, active listening, peer teaching, vocabulary building, visualisation, and best of all, enjoyment.

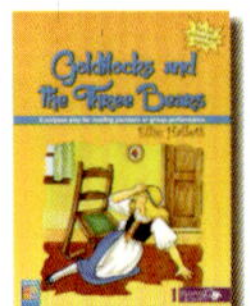

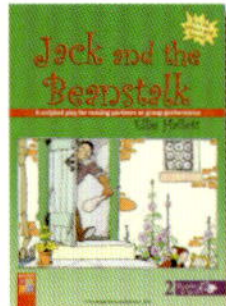

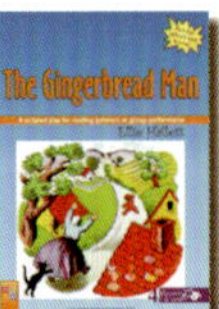

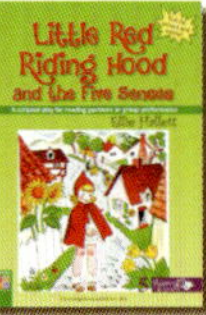

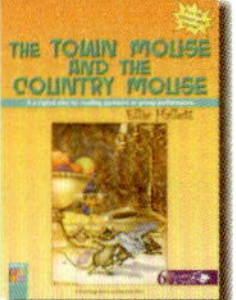

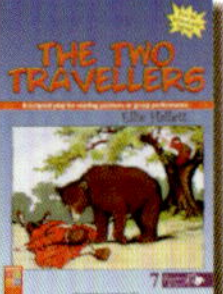

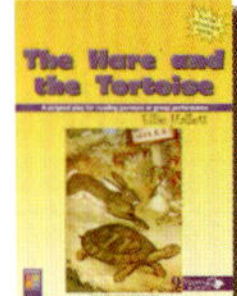

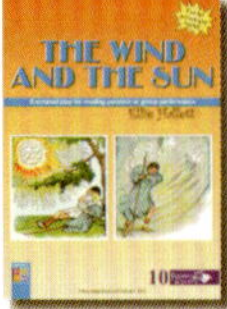

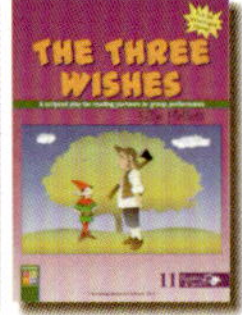

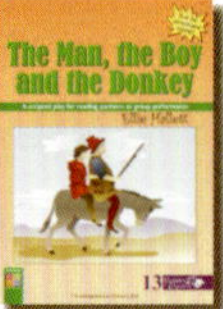

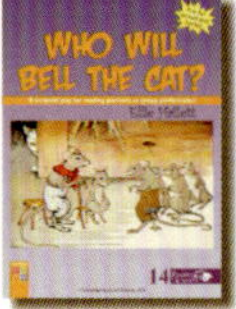

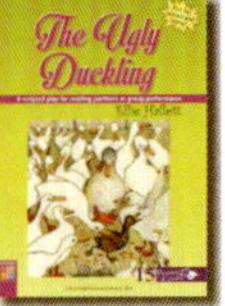

ISBN	Title	Author	Price	E-book Price	QTY
9781921016455	Goldilocks and The Three Bears	Hallett, Ellie	9.95	9.95	
9781925398045	Jack and the Beanstalk	Hallett, Ellie	9.95	9.95	
9781925398069	The Fox and the Goat	Hallett, Ellie	9.95	9.95	
9781925398076	The Gingerbread Man	Hallett, Ellie	9.95	9.95	
9781925398052	Little Red Riding Hood and the Five Senses	Hallett, Ellie	9.95	9.95	
9781925398083	The Town Mouse and the Country Mouse	Hallett, Ellie	9.95	9.95	
9781925398014	The Two Travellers	Hallett, Ellie	9.95	9.95	
9781925398007	The Enormous Turnip	Hallett, Ellie	9.95	9.95	
9781925398090	The Hare and the Tortoise	Hallett, Ellie	9.95	9.95	
9781925398106	The Wind and the Sun	Hallett, Ellie	9.95	9.95	
9781925398113	The Three Wishes	Hallett, Ellie	9.95	9.95	
9781921016554	The Man, the Boy and the Donkey	Hallett, Ellie	9.95	9.95	
9781925398120	The Fox and the Crow	Hallett, Ellie	9.95	9.95	
9781920824921	Who Will Bell the Cat?	Hallett, Ellie	9.95	9.95	
9781925398021	The Ugly Duckling	Hallett, Ellie	9.95	9.95	

www.kbs.com.au